HAUDENOSAUNEE

Heather Bruegl

21st Century Junior Library

Indigenous Peoples of North America

Published in the United States of America by:

Cherry Lake Press
2395 South Huron Parkway, Suite 200, Ann Arbor, Michigan 48104
www.cherrylakepress.com

Reading Adviser: Beth Walker Gambro, MS, Ed., Reading Consultant, Yorkville, IL

Photo Credits: U.S. Army Photo by Maj. Dave Hoy, cover and title page; © fandangle/Shutterstock, 5; © EWY Media/Shutterstock, 6; © Brett Zimmerman/Shutterstock, 8; © Vespasian/Alamy Stock Photo, 9; (c) History and Art Collection/Alamy Stock Photo, 11; © ASSOCIATED PRESS, 13; © Paul Massie Photography/Shutterstock, 14; AnnaJB/ Wikimedia Commons via CC BY-SA 4.0, 17; © ZUMA Press, Inc./Alamy Stock Photo, 19; National Museum of the American Indian, Smithsonian Institute, Photo by David Grant Noble, 21

Cherry Lake Press is an imprint of Cherry Lake Publishing Group.

Library of Congress Cataloging-in-Publication Data

Names: Bruegl, Heather, author.
Title: Haudenosaunee / written by: Heather Bruegl.
Description: Ann Arbor, MI : Cherry Lake Publishing, [2025] | Series: Indigenous peoples of North America | Includes bibliographical references and index. | Audience: Grades 2-3 | Summary: "The Haudenosaunee peoples, sometimes called the Iroquois, share language, culture, and history that connects them in many ways in both the United States and Canada. In this introduction to the People of the Longhouse, readers will learn about the Mohawk, Oneida, Onondaga, Cayuga, Seneca, and Tuscarora peoples, lands, history, and accomplishments. Written by Indigenous author and public historian, Heather Bruegl, a citizen of the Oneida Nation and first-line descendent Strockbridge-Munsee, this series provides a simple and authentic introduction to the unique cultures and peoples that have made this continent home for thousands of years, and are still here today"– Provided by publisher.
Identifiers: LCCN 2024036519 | ISBN 9781668956298 (hardcover) | ISBN 9781668957141 (paperback) | ISBN 9781668958018 (ebook) | ISBN 9781668958889 (pdf)
Subjects: LCSH: Iroquois Indians–History–Juvenile literature. | Five Nations–Juvenile literature. | Six Nations–Juvenile literature.
Classification: LCC E99.I7 B88 2025 | DDC 974.7004/9755–dc23/eng/20240923
LC record available at https://lccn.loc.gov/2024036519

Cherry Lake Publishing would like to acknowledge the work of the Partnership for 21st Century Learning, a network of Battelle for Kids. Please visit Battelle for Kids online for more information.

Printed in the United States of America

Note from publisher: Websites change regularly, and their future contents are outside of our control. Supervise children when conducting any recommended online searches for extended learning opportunities.

About the Cover: Retired Command Sergeant Major Ron Cook Jr. of the Seneca Nation is pictured here participating in the U.S. Military Academy's Native American Heritage Forum's second annual Eagle Feather Gifting Ceremony at West Point. One of the recipients was Cadet Brock Hinkle of the Mohawk Nation. Cook served in the 82nd Airborne Division and made a combat jump into Panama. Cook represents the proud history of Haudenosaunee military service.

CONTENTS

WHO WE ARE

Haudenosaunee means "People of the Long House." It is a group of tribal nations that share similar languages and traditions. Each nation has its own name with its own meaning. Each also has its own language and traditions.

The Haudenosaunee formed a **confederacy**. Five nations with unique cultures and traditions joined. They were the Mohawk, Oneida, Onondaga, Cayuga, and Seneca. They joined under the Great Law of Peace. This agreement gave important roles to each nation. They were called the Five Nations Confederacy.

Look!

Look at the Haudenosaunee flag. What do you notice? How does it show unity? What do you notice about the symbol in the center?

In 1722, the Tuscarora joined them. They had traveled north seeking safety. They added another layer of cultural richness to the Haudenosaunee. The Confederacy then became the Six Nations.

The Haudenosaunee recorded treaties and important events on wampum belts. Wampum are beads made out of shells.

Make a Guess!

Many know the Haudenosaunee by the name *Iroquois*. *Iroquois* means "black snake" in the Huron, or Wyandot, language. Why do you think this book is called *Haudenosaunee* and not *Iroquois*?

The original Confederacy ended at the time of the **American Revolution** (1775–1783). The nations chose different paths. But the teachings of the Great Law of Peace continue. Members of the Six Nations Confederacy still live by these values and beliefs.

The longhouse was central to Haudenosaunee life. Extended families lived together. They worked together. Strong families are part of who they are.

The Haudenosaunee nations value shared labor and strong family relationships. They believe in being **stewards** of the land. Their values also include wisdom and foresight. The Haudenosaunee believe that all decisions should benefit people for seven generations. This is especially true of land use and protection.

Haudenosaunee traditions and values are passed down to each new generation.

OUR LIVES TODAY

Today, large numbers of Haudenosaunee people live in New York state. Tens of thousands live in Canada. Some of their ancestors experienced **forced relocation** by the U.S. government. Large populations of Oneida moved to Wisconsin. The Seneca and Cayuga were relocated to Oklahoma. Their communities are still active and thriving in those places.

Think!

How might life be different in places like New York, Wisconsin, and Oklahoma?

Notable people of the Haudenosaunee include Oneida activist Laura Cornelius Kellogg, Cayuga actor Gary Farmer, and Seneca author John Mohawk. Many

Laura Cornelius Kellogg (1880–1947) helped set the stage for the next 100 years of progress in Indigenous rights.

great leaders have led the tribal nations through wars and removals.

Haudenosaunee social structures continue to be important in tribal life. **Clan mothers** hold positions of great respect and influence. They help preserve culture and reclaim the language.

Like many tribal nations, the Haudenosaunee are working to reclaim their traditions, culture, language, and land. These projects are a reclamation of life before **colonization**. The Onondaga worked to get the U.S. government to return 1,000 acres (405 hectares) of **unceded land**. The government agreed to do this in 2022. Efforts like this help Haudenosaunee nations uphold their commitment to the land and future.

Tadodaho Sidney Hill represented the Onondaga Council of Chiefs and Clan Mothers in the 2022 land return. The title *Tadodaho* is given to the Onondaga spiritual leader.

OUR ANCESTRAL LANDS

The Haudenosaunee lived mainly in the eastern United States and Canada. That land is now in the state of New York and the provinces of Ottawa and Quebec.

Each member nation had its own territory. The Seneca lived the farthest west. The Mohawk lived the farthest east. Both nations defended the Confederacy's outer borders. The Onondaga lands were in the center. The Great Tree of Peace, the symbol of the Confederacy, stood there. The other member nations' lands were on either side of the Onondaga.

Haudenosaunee land was rich in resources. Each season brought different natural gifts used for food, clothing, and medicines. Resources were gathered and stored for use during the year.

The Haudenosaunee were expert farmers. They farmed in the **Three Sisters** method. They grew corn, beans, and squash. These foods provided needed nutrients. The people also hunted game such as deer, wild turkeys, and geese. Every part of an animal was used for food, clothing, or tools. Nothing was wasted. Plants were used for food and medicine. Everything and everyone played a part.

Create!

Make a collage of images of the Three Sisters: corn, beans, and squash. Find images in magazines or go online with an adult and print them. Include a caption that tells how these foods are still important today.

Haudenosaunee farmers still use traditional planting methods today.

CARRYING TRADITIONS FORWARD

Life changed greatly for many Haudenosaunee after the U.S. government relocated them. They had to rebuild far from their homeland. They were denied their traditions and ability to **self-govern**. This was true of all tribal nations across North America.

The Haudenosaunee refused to be defeated. Instead, they **persevered**. They held onto their family bonds and many traditions like beadwork and lacrosse. They learned to help their communities in different ways.

HAUDENOSAUNEE
4

Ironworkers were needed as cities grew. Many Haudenosaunee people took these jobs. They built a bridge over the St. Lawrence River in 1886. By the 1910s, many Haudenosaunee were working on some of the tallest skyscrapers of that time! You can see their work in New York City. They helped build the George Washington Bridge, the Empire State Building, and the United Nations Headquarters.

Today, the Haudenosaunee work to bring back their traditions and language. They also work to reclaim the land they were forced to leave. Many communities have tribal museums and tell their stories in ways that matter to them.

Jay Jacobs and Sparky Rice were two Mohawk ironworkers in New York City.

Ask Questions!

What more would you like to know about the Haudenosaunee nations? Ask a teacher, librarian, or other adult to help you find answers.

GLOSSARY

American Revolution (**uh-MAIR-uh-kuhn reh-vuh-LOO-shuhn**) the war for independence fought between the United States and Great Britain

clan mothers (**KLAN MUH-therz**) positions of respect and responsibility held by women in some Indigenous social structures; Haudenosaunee clan mothers choose the chiefs and carry on the language and culture to the next generations

colonization (**kah-luh-nuh-ZAY-shuhn**) the act of settling in an area and exercising control over Indigenous people

confederacy (**kuhn-FEH-druh-see**) a group of people or nations joined for a common purpose

forced relocation (**FORST ree-loh-KAY-shuhn**) involuntary movement of people through the use of threats or military action

persevered (**puhr-suh-VEERD**) overcame difficult challenges

self-govern (**self-GUH-vern**) the ability to rule your own nation

stewards (**STOO-erdz**) caretakers

Three Sisters (**THREE SIH-sterz**) a form of planting in Indigenous communities that refers to the planting of corn, beans, and squash

unceded land (**uhn-SEE-ded LAND**) land that was not given up with a sale or treaty

FIND OUT MORE

Books

Bruegl, Heather. *Longhouse Form of Government*. Ann Arbor, MI: Cherry Lake Press, 2024.

Shoulders, Michael and Debbie Shoulders. *D is for Drum: A Native American Alphabet*. Ann Arbor, MI: Sleeping Bear Press, 2006.

Sorell, Traci. *We Are Still Here! Native American Truths Everyone Should Know*. Watertown, MA: Charlesbridge, 2021.

Online

With an adult, explore more online with these suggested searches.

- "History," Onondaga Nation
- "Our Heritage," Seneca-Iroquois National Museum

Say Hello!

Nya:wëh sgë:nö' (NYAH-weh SKAY-no) is a Seneca greeting that means "I am grateful you are well."

INDEX

ABOUT THE AUTHOR

Heather Bruegl, a member of the Oneida Nation of Wisconsin/Stockbridge-Munsee, is a Madonna University graduate with a Master of Arts in U.S. History. She is a public historian and decolonial educator, and her Munsee name is Kiishookunkwe, which means "Sunflower in Full Bloom." Heather frequently travels to present on Indigenous history, policy, and activism, bringing her deep knowledge and personal connection to the subject.